Lun

The
Cherokee Indians

by Bill Lund

Reading Consultant:
Cliff Trafzer, Ph.D.
Professor of Native American Studies
Director of Costo Historical and Linguistics
Native American Research Center

Bridgestone Books
an Imprint of Capstone Press

Bridgestone Books are published by Capstone Press
818 North Willow Street, Mankato, Minnesota 56001
Copyright © 1997 by Capstone Press
All rights reserved
Printed in the United States of America

Library of Congress Cataloging-in-Publication Data
Lund, Bill, 1954-
      The Cherokee Indians/by Bill Lund.
            p. cm.--(Native peoples)
      Includes bibliographical references and index.
      Summary: Provides an overview of the past and present lives of the
Cherokee people, covering their daily life, customs, relations with
the government and others, and more.
      ISBN 1-56065-477-5
      1. Cherokee Indians--Juvenile literature. [1. Cherokee Indians.
2. Indians of North America--Oklahoma. 3. Indians of North America-
-Southern States.]   I. Title. II. Series: Lund, Bill, 1954-
Native peoples.
E99.C5L93   1997
973'.049755--dc21
                                                          96-39767
                                                            CIP
                                                              AC

Photo credits
Bettmann Archive, 18; Cliff Owen, 10
Florida Department of Tourism, 16
FPG, 20
International Stock/Phyllis Picardi, cover
Unicorn/Robert Ginn, 6, Phyllis Kedl, 8; Paul Murphy, 12;
   Jean Higgins, 14

Table of Contents

Map

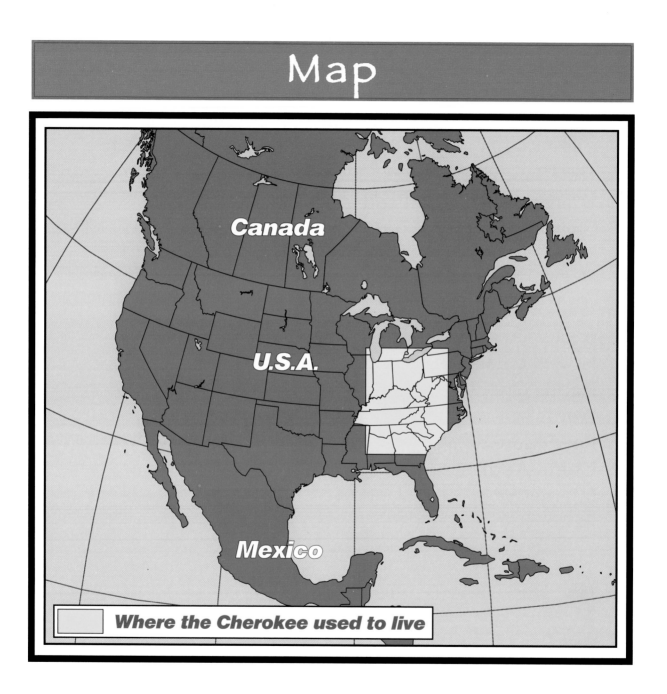

Canada

U.S.A.

Mexico

Where the Cherokee used to live

Fast Facts

Today many Cherokee Indians live like most other North Americans. In the past, they practiced a different way of life. Their food, homes, and clothes helped make them special. These facts tell how Cherokees once lived.

Food: Cherokees grew corn, squash, and beans. They hunted deer, elk, fox, and bear. They also fished.

Home: They lived in round houses made of wood. The wood was covered with plaster made of mud and grass. The roofs were made of bark.

Clothing: Cherokee men wore a breechcloth. This was a piece of deerskin. It passed between the legs. It was tied with a belt. Men also wore deerskin shirts. Women wore deerskin tops and skirts.

Language: Cherokees spoke their own Cherokee language.

Past Location: Cherokee land covered parts of Tennessee, North Carolina, South Carolina, Virginia, West Virginia, Kentucky, Georgia, Alabama, and Arkansas.

Current Location: Today most Cherokees live in North Carolina and Oklahoma. Many live in U.S. cities.

Special Events: Cherokees held many feasts and dances. These honored different things. Some were Green Corn, Harvest, and Strawberry.

The Cherokee Nation

Today the Cherokee Nation is one of the largest Indian nations. A nation is a group of people. These people have the same language and government. Nearly 60,000 Cherokees live in the United States.

Many North American Indian groups live together as a nation. Sometimes they live together on a reservation. A reservation is land set aside for use by Native Americans.

The Cherokee Nation is different. It is split in two. Most Cherokees live in northeastern Oklahoma. They live and work as part of their communities. Some Cherokees live on North Carolina's Cherokee reservation.

Cherokee people live and work in a modern world. But they also try to remember their old way of life. They still practice their own language, art, and religion. A religion is a set of beliefs people follow.

The Cherokee are keeping their old way of life alive.

Village, Home, and Food

In the past, Cherokees lived in villages. The most important building was the Council House. The Council House was in the center of the village. Cherokees held important meetings there.

Cherokee families built their homes around the Council House. The homes were built of wood. The wood was covered inside and out with plaster. The plaster was made of mud and grass. The roof was made of tree bark.

Inside, houses were decorated with colorful rugs and baskets. Cherokees used buffalo robes and animal skins for beds. They made chairs out of tree bark.

Each home had a fire burning in the center. Smoke escaped through a hole in the roof. Women cooked meals over the fire.

Corn was a popular Cherokee food. It was made into corn mush. This was like soup. Deer, rabbits, and turkeys were other foods.

In the past, Cherokees lived in villages.

Cherokee Women

Women have always had an important place in Cherokee life. Today that place is more important than ever.

Cherokee women have always had a part in Cherokee government. They have made decisions for their people.

In the past, Cherokee women chose their husbands. Sometimes the husband built a house for his wife. Other times he lived with his wife's family. Women owned the house and all the property. Women also had control of the children.

In the past, women were warriors, too. A warrior is a brave fighter. Women warriors were called Pretty Women or War Women.

Today women are leaders in the Cherokee Nation. Wilma Mankiller is a well-known woman. She was elected Principal Chief of the Oklahoma Cherokee Nation in 1985. She was the first woman to hold that office.

Wilma Mankiller was elected Principal Chief in 1985.

Clans and Chiefs

The Cherokee Nation is divided into seven clans. Clans are large family groups. Each person is a member of a clan.

Clan membership comes from the mother. Each child becomes a member of the mother's clan.

Each village had a chief. The right-hand man and the speaker helped the chief. They sat next to the chief in the Council House. Six other men helped rule, too. They were called the council. They made laws and led special events.

Things changed when the Cherokee went to war. Then another chief and his men took charge. These men ruled during war time. When the Cherokee made peace, the war-time chief stopped ruling. The peace-time chief ruled again.

The Cherokee Nation was ruled in the same way. It had a chief and a council. They made important decisions for the Cherokee Nation.

Cherokees were ruled by chiefs.

Shamans

Cherokee religion honored things in nature. Long ago, Cherokees believed that objects in nature had spirits. They often prayed to the spirits for strength and help. Some Cherokees still have these beliefs.

Sometimes Cherokees would wear or sleep on animal skins. They hoped they would receive the skills of those animals.

Shamans were once important in the Cherokee religion. A shaman is a religious leader. Both women and men could be shamans.

Shamans knew special prayers and songs. They knew how to heal people with herbs and tree barks.

Cherokees respected shamans. People went to see shamans if they had problems. They paid the shamans for help. Many Cherokees still visit shamans.

Sometimes Cherokees would wear animal skins.

THE TRAIL OF TEARS

Kansas	Missouri	Illinois	Indiana	Ohio
				West Virginia
			Kentucky	
				Virginia
Oklahoma	Arkansas		Tennessee	North Carolina
				South Carolina
Texas	Mississippi	Alabama	Georgia	

Water Route   Land Route

16

Trail of Tears

The Cherokee used to live in eastern North America. But today most live in Oklahoma. They moved to Oklahoma on the Trail of Tears.

The U.S. government wanted the Cherokee's land in the east. It passed the Indian Removal Act in 1830. This allowed the government to force Indians from their lands.

Many Cherokees were against this. They took their case to the U.S. Supreme Court. The court said the government could not move the Cherokee. But the government did anyway.

President Andrew Jackson used the U.S. Army. The army captured all the Cherokees they could find. They forced them to move to Oklahoma.

Most Cherokees had to walk the entire distance. They walked through cold, heat, and rain. More than 4,000 Cherokees died on the journey. This is why it is called the Trail of Tears.

Andrew Jackson forced Cherokees from their lands.

Baskets and Jars

Cherokees created many objects of art. They made things for decoration. They also made things to help with daily jobs.

Cherokee women are known for their basket weaving. They use plants and vines to make baskets. Many of their baskets have fancy designs. Cherokees paint baskets, too. In the past, they made paints out of plants.

Cherokees made pots, jars, and bowls from clay. Many objects were decorated with patterns and colorful designs. Cherokees kept grains and other food in big jars. Others were used for cooking.

Cherokee men were skilled at carving wood. They made wood into shapes and designs. They carved canoes, pipes, and tools. Many Cherokee men, women, and children create art today.

Cherokees make baskets from plants and vines.

How the Earth Began

Cherokees have special stories that are called legends. Sometimes these stories explain things that happen in nature. This Cherokee story explains how the earth began.

Once the world was all water. Animals and people lived in the world above. It was very crowded in the world above. So Water Beetle decided to see what he could do.

Water Beetle went down into the water. He swam all around. He dived to the bottom of the water. He saw mud down there. He grabbed some in his mouth.

Water Beetle swam to the top of the water. He spit the mud out of his mouth. The mud began to spread and grow. Soon it became an island. The animals named it earth.

The animals and people waited for the earth to dry. Then they left the crowded world above. They moved to earth.

A Cherokee legend says once the world was all water.

Hands On: Play Hoop and Pole

Playing hoop and pole was popular among Cherokee men and boys. This game helped improve their throwing skills.

What You Need
One hula hoop
One long stick per player

What You Do
1. Choose a person to roll the hula hoop. Roll the hula hoop so that the circle faces the players.
2. While the hoop is rolling, try to throw the stick through the hoop.
3. Roll the hoop five times.
4. The person with the most throws through the hoop wins.

Words to Know

clan (KLAN)—a large family group
Council House (KOUN-suhl HOUSS)—a building in the center of a Cherokee village where important meetings were held
legend (LEJ-uhnd)—a special story that explains things in nature
reservation (rez-ur-VAY-shuhn)—land set aside for use by Native Americans
shaman (SHAH-men)—a respected religious man or woman who knows special songs and prayers; he or she also knows how to heal people with herbs.

Read More

Landau, Elaine. *The Cherokees*. New York: Franklin Watts, 1992.
Sneve, Virginia Driving Hawk. *The Cherokees*. New York: Holiday House, 1996.

Useful Addresses

Cherokee of Oklahoma
P.O. Box 948
Tahlequah, OK 74465

United Keetoowah Band of Cherokee
2450 South Muskogee Avenue
Tahlequah, OK 74464

Internet Sites

Codetalk Home Page
http://www.codetalk.fed.us/home.html

Native American Indian
http://indy4.fdl.cc.mn.us/~isk/

Index